*Mandukya Upanishad
and Commentary*

By
Charles Johnston

Copyright © 2021 Lamp of Trismegistus. All rights reserved. No part of this publication may be reproduced or transmitted in any form or by any means, electronic or mechanical, including photocopying, recording, or by any information storage and retrieval system, without permission in writing from Lamp of Trismegistus. Reviewers may quote brief passages.

ISBN: 978-1-63118-497-0

Esoteric Classics:
Eastern Studies

Other Books in this Series and Related Titles

Isha Upanishad and Commentary by Charles Johnston (978-1-63118-490-1)

Kena Upanishad and Commentary by Charles Johnston (978-1-63118-491-8)

Katha Upanishad and Commentary by Charles Johnston (978-1-63118-493-2)

Prashna Upanishad and Commentary by Charles Johnston (978-1-63118-494-9)

Mundaka Upanishad and Commentary by Charles Johnston (978-1-63118-496-3)

Atma Bodha & Tattva Bodha by Adi Shankara &c (978-1-63118-401-7)

The Crest-Jewel of Wisdom by Adi Shankara (978-1-63118-475-8)

The Book of Wisdom of Solomon by King Solomon (978-1-63118-502-1)

Catholicism, Yoga and Hinduism by Hartmann &c (978-1-63118-478-9)

Yoga, Hatha-Yoga and Raja-Yoga by Annie Besant (978-1-63118-476-5)

The Tree of Wisdom by Nagarjuna (978-1-63118-470-3)

The Path of Light: A Manual of Maha-Yana Buddhism (978-1-63118-471-0)

Buddhist Psalms by Shinran (978-1-63118-465-9)

Tao Te Ching & Commentary by Lao Tzu & C Johnston (978-1-63118-495-6)

The Hymns of Hermes by G. R. S. Mead (978-1-63118-405-5)

The Golden Verses of Pythagoras: Five Translations (978-1-63118-479-6)

Gnosis of the Mind by G. R. S. Mead (978-1-63118-408-6)

The Hymn of Jesus by G. R. S. Mead (978-1-63118-492-5)

The Book of the Watchers by Enoch (978-1-63118-416-1)

The Secrets of Enoch by Enoch (978-1-63118-449-9)

A Collection of Early Writings on Astral Travel (978-1-63118-477-2)

Audio versions are also available on Audible, Amazon and Apple

Other Books in this Series and Related Titles

Alchemy in the Nineteenth Century by Helena P. Blavatsky (978-1-63118-446-8)

The Influence of Pythagoras on Freemasonry and Other Essays (978-1-63118-404-8)

The Mysteries of Freemasonry & the Druids by A Mackey &c (978-1-63118-444-4)

The Rosicrucian Chemical Marriage by Christian Rosenkreuz (978-1-63118-458-1)

Ancient Mysteries and Secret Societies by M P Hall (978-1-63118-410-9)

Masonic and Rosicrucian History by M P Hall & H Voorhis (978-1-63118-486-4)

History, Analysis and Secret Tradition of the Tarot by Hall &c (978-1-63118-445-1)

The First and Second Gospels of the Infancy of Jesus Christ by Thomas and James (978-1-63118-415-4)

The Kabbalah of Masonry & Related Writings by E Levi &c (978-1-63118-453-6)

The Poem of Hashish by A Crowley & C Baudelaire (978-1-63118-484-0)

Crystal Vision Through Crystal Gazing by Frater Achad (978-1-63118-455-0)

Fortune-Telling with Dice by Astra Cielo (978-1-63118-466-6)

The Human Aura: Astral Colors and Thought Forms (978-1-63118-419-2)

The Master Mason's Handbook by J S M Ward (978-1-63118-474-1)

The Legend of the Holy Grail and its Connection with Templars and Freemasons by A E Waite (978-1-63118-462-8)

Cloud Upon the Sanctuary by A E Waite & K Eckartshausen (978-1-63118-438-3)

The Feminine Occult by various authors (978-1-63118-711-7)

Magical Essays and Instructions by Florence Farr (978-1-63118-418-5)

The Path of Light: A Manual of Maha-Yana Buddhism (978-1-63118-471-0)

Arcane Formulas or Mental Alchemy by W W Atkinson (978-1-63118-459-8)

Audio versions are also available on Audible, Amazon and Apple

Table of Contents

Introduction…7

Mandukya Upanishad
Translated by Charles Johnston…9

The Measure of the Eternal
Commentary on the Mandukya Upanishad
By Charles Johnston…13

Natural Psychical and Spiritual Bodies
Gaudapada's Poem on the Mandukya Upanishad
Translated by Charles Johnston…23

INTRODUCTION

The word "esoteric" can be difficult to define. Esotericism in general can be seen less as a system of beliefs and more as a category, which encompasses numerous, different systems of beliefs. It's a bit of juxtaposition, since the word "esoteric" indicates something that few people know about, while the term itself broadly covers numerous philosophies, practices, areas of study and belief systems.

In a greater sense, Esotericism acts as a storehouse for secret knowledge, which is often considered ancient (*by tradition, if not by fact*), passed down from generation to generation, in private. At various times in history, simply possessing the knowledge of some of these subjects, was considered illegal and a jailable offence, if discovered. This usually included such general topics as Alchemy, Pharmacology, Qabalah, Hermeticism, Occultism, Ceremonial Magic, Astrology, Divination, Rosicrucianism and so on. Collectively, these areas of study were often referred to as the esoteric sciences.

Sometimes, the outer garment of a subject isn't esoteric, while what is hidden beneath it, is. As an example, Freemasonry isn't necessarily esoteric by nature (at *least not anymore*), but certain signs, passwords and handshakes given to the candidate during their initiation, are in fact, esoteric, in the sense that they are hidden from the general public.

Today, in the twenty-first century, such topics are readily available at bookstores across the country, and numerous mainsteam publishers offer beginners guides and coffee-table volumes on many of these subjects, intended for mass appeal. Books like *"The Secret"* have turned previously arcane topics into household knowledge. All that being the case, however, it isn't to say that there still aren't buried secrets to uncover, ancient wisdom being ignored and forgotten mysteries to be explored. In fact, it is often that we are only able to further our own studies by standing on the shoulders of these disappearing giants.

Lamp of Trismegistus is doing its part to help preserve humanity's esoteric history by making some of these classics available to those students who are seeking to unearth the knowledge of these ancient colossi.

So, be sure to check other titles from our *Esoteric Classics* series, as well as our *Occult Fiction, Theosophical Classics, Eastern Studies, Foundations of Freemasonry Series, Supernatural Fiction, Paranormal Research Series, Studies in Buddhism* and our *Christian Apocrypha Series.* You can also download the audio versions of most of these titles from Amazon, Apple or Audible, for learning on the go.

MANDUKYA UPANISHAD

Translated by Charles Johnston

"'Om': This imperishable syllable is all that is. Its expansive expression is: What has been, What is, What shall be. All this is 'Om.' And whatever else there is, beyond the threefold division of Time, that, also, verily, is 'Om.' For all this is Brahma, the Eternal; and the Self, Atma, is the Eternal. And this Self stands in four worlds.

"In the world of Waking Consciousness, *Jagrat*, objectively perceiving, of sevenfold form, with nineteen mouths – organs of sense and action – an enjoyer of gross matter, this is the Natural Self, *Vaishvanara*, the first measure or foot.

"In the world of Dream Consciousness, *Swapna*, subjectively perceiving, of sevenfold form, with nineteen mouths – organs of sense and action – an enjoyer of finer matter, this is the Psychical Self, *Taijasa*, the second measure or foot.

"Where, entered into rest, he desires no desire and beholds no dream, this is Dreamless Consciousness, *Sushupti*. Dreamless consciousness, unified, collective perception, verily, made of bliss, an enjoyer of bliss, perceiving through the heart, this is the Spiritual Self, *Prajna*, the third measure or foot. This is the All-lord, this is the all-knower, this is the Inner ruler, this is the womb of all, the forthcoming and indrawing of beings.

"Neither subjectively perceiving, nor objectively perceiving, nor perceiving in both ways, neither collective perception, nor perception nor non-perception; unseen, not to be apprehended, not to be grasped, without sign of separation, unimaginable, unindicable, the essence of the consciousness of the Self, in which the manifest world ceases, full of peace, benign, secondless, this is held to be the Fourth Consciousness, this is the Self, *Atma*, this is the goal of wisdom.

"This Self, Atma, corresponds according to syllables with the 'Om' according to its measures. The measures are as the feet, and the feet are as the measures: A, U and M, to wit.

"The Natural Self in Waking Consciousness, is the A, the first measure, so called from being the first, and from acquiring. He passes beyond all desires and becomes first, who thus knows,

"The Psychical Self, in Dream Consciousness, is the U, the second measure, so called from its up-raising and uniting. He is upraised to the highest knowledge, and becomes united, nor in his family do knowers of the Eternal fail, who thus knows.

"The Spiritual Self in Dreamless Consciousness, is the M, the third measure, so called because it measures all, or because all merges in it. He measures all, and in him all merges, who thus knows.

"Without measure is the Fourth, not to be apprehended, wherein manifestation comes to rest, the benign, secondless.

Thus the 'Om' is as the Self, Mind. Through the Self, he enters the Self, who thus knows, who thus knows."

THE MEASURE OF THE ETERNAL

MANDUKYA Upanishad

Translated from the Sanskrit with an Interpretation

Om: this syllable, this imperishable, is the All. Its expansion is what has been, what is, what shall be. All, verily, is Om. And whatsoever else surpasses the three times, this also is Om. For all this is the Eternal, this is the Divine Self; and this Divine Self has four measures.

Standing in waking, outwardly perceiving, of sevenfold form, with nineteen energies, experiencing the gross, Common-to-all-men, this is the first measure.

Standing in dream, inwardly perceiving, of sevenfold form, with nineteen energies, experiencing the subtle, the Radiant, this is the second measure.

Where entering into rest, he desires no desire, nor beholds any dream, this is dreamlessness. Standing in dreamlessness, unified, a sphere of spiritual perception, formed of joy, experiencing joy, whose energy is spiritual consciousness, the Wise Seer is the third measure. He is Lord of all, he is all-knowing, he is the inner ruler, he is the source of all, the forth-going and the indrawing of lives.

Nor outwardly perceiving, nor inwardly perceiving, nor perceiving in both ways, nor a sphere of spiritual perception, nor perception, nor non-perception; invisible, inapprehensible, ungraspable, indistinguishable, unimaginable, unindicable, whose essence is realization of oneness with the Eternal, where forth-going is ended, still, benign, beyond duality, is held to be the fourth; this is the Divine Self, this is the goal of wisdom.

The Mandukya, briefest and yet most inclusive of all the great Upanishads, undertakes to describe the universe in terms of consciousness and of vehicles of consciousness in four progressive degrees. There is only a passing indication of the objective world presented to consciousness through these degrees.

The philosophical justification of this treatment is the truth that consciousness is the one thing we know at first hand; objects we know only as they are reflected in consciousness. That we should ever know objects as they are in themselves, that is, unrelated to consciousness, appears to be impossible, a contradiction in terms; though we may and without doubt shall come to know them as they present themselves to a deeper and more real consciousness, thus knowing them more truly.

Science undertakes to describe objects as they are in themselves; but in reality science does not so describe them, since all observation rests on the impressions which objects make on consciousness, whether immediately, through the senses, or mediately, through various instruments like the microscope or telescope, which are simply extensions of the lenses of the eyes. All scientific observation, therefore, consists of the impressions which objects make on what we may call the outer layer of consciousness; while all scientific interpretation is derived from certain deeper powers of consciousness, powers of which science, even while continually and consistently using them, gives no real account, but simply takes them for granted.

Science uses reason to reach its conclusions, and often uses it with admirable power; yet science does not appear to have begun by establishing the necessarily precedent thesis, that reason is reasonable, that it may be depended on to reach truth. That is taken for granted, to a large degree quite unconsciously, with no very clear realization that the problem exists. The truth would seem to be that this conviction that reason is a trustworthy guide is itself derived from consciousness, from a deeper layer than the layer which reasons, a layer which we may call intuitional.

Science thus depends on sensuous consciousness for its observations, on rational consciousness for its interpretations and, if we are right, on intuitional consciousness for the validation both of sense perception and of the process of reasoning.

We may, perhaps, postulate a form of consciousness even deeper than intuition, a consciousness from which we draw the conviction that there is a universe to experience and interpret, the consciousness of Being itself.

The philosophical justification for describing the universe in terms of consciousness is, then, the simple fact that there is no other way in which we can describe it. It is all a question of our consciousness, and of what our consciousness contains. This is the beginning. There is no indication of a possible end.

The Mandukya Upanishad describes consciousness as one, made manifest in four degrees, with appropriate vehicles. But form or shape, as we experience it in our ordinary life, is present only in the first two of the four degrees. The third and fourth are above form in that sense. There is, therefore, a medial line; below it is the realm of form, while above it principles or potencies take the place of form.

The idea of conscious experience devoid of form by no means takes us beyond what we already know. Take music, for example, a very rich and abounding field of experience. As music reaches our consciousness, it has no form or shape, in the sense that a picture, or a statue, or a building has form or shape. Yet we are clearly conscious in music of a quality which corresponds to architectural form, like that, let us say, of the Parthenon, or of a quality which corresponds to beauty of colour. And all music rests on the truth that it can and does render a great realm of our experience. And this it does without shape or form in the ordinary sense. So that we are familiar with one very rich realm of consciousness which is independent of form. We may, therefore, form a concept, however inadequate, of a realm accessible to conscious, in which reality is manifested without form as we experience it; in which powers and principles take the place of form: the realm above the medial line.

To come back to the text of the Mandukya. The first paragraph outlines the unity of the universe, the unmanifest All and its manifestation; the universe in eternity, and its manifestation in the three times, past, present, future. The Eternal, the Divine Self, is made manifest in four realms, four ranges of consciousness; if we wish to find more definite terms, we may, perhaps, speak of these four degrees as that of the man, the disciple, the adept and the Mahatma. The first two are described in terms of form; the third and fourth, in terms of principles or powers. The third and fourth are above the medial line, above Maya.

The second paragraph describes the vehicle of the consciousness of the man, the physical body. It is sevenfold: head, upper and lower trunk, the four limbs. It has nineteen energies; namely, five senses or powers of perception, five powers of action, five vital breaths, to which are added mind (Manas), imagination (Chitta), the personal sense (Ahankara), and intelligence (Buddhi).

This vehicle with its range of consciousness is called Common-to-all-men (Vaishvanara); it is described as standing in waking consciousness; perceiving outwardly, and experiencing the gross; that is, having the experience of ordinary physical life.

The second vesture or vehicle of consciousness is called the Radiant (Taijasa). *The Theosophical Glossary* says that this term is used "to designate the Manasarupa, the 'thought-body.'" The vesture called the Radiant would appear to be what *Light on the Path* calls the astral body. Both words mean "starry." The Mandukya describes it as a subtile counterpart of the natural body; like it, possessing form and members, and with a range of corresponding powers. It is said to stand in dream; that is, a consciousness of forms, perhaps a four-dimensional consciousness.

The third vesture appears to be what Shankaracharya calls the causal body, of which *The Theosophical Glossary* says: "This 'body,' which is no body either objective or subjective, but Buddhi, the Spiritual Soul, is so called because it is the direct cause of the Sushupti condition, leading to the Turiya state." We have translated Sushupti by "dreamlessness," a consciousness above form. Therefore the causal body (Karana sharira) is the vesture of a consciousness and a range of powers, which we have suggested may be the consciousness and powers of the adept. Of this consciousness, the Mandukya says that it is "unified, a sphere of spiritual perception, formed of joy, experiencing joy, whose energy is spiritual consciousness (Chetas)." And to this vesture with its consciousness is given the name "the Wise Seer" (Prajna). He is the Lord of all, all-knowing, the inner ruler. The concluding phrases of this paragraph: "the source of all, the forth-going and indrawing of lives," refer to the causal body, which, according to Shankaracharya, is "the cause and substance of the two other bodies," sending them forth in the series of lives, and, when each life is completed, drawing back the spiritual substance and force into itself; in this sense, the inner ruler of the whole series of lives.

The word Turiya, already cited, which is applied to the higher of the two ranges of spiritual consciousness above the realm of form, is simply the ordinal number, "fourth." That consciousness is called by the Mandukya "Atma," which we have rendered "Divine Self." It appears to be a consciousness beyond individuality, which is in one sense the most fundamental thing in our present experience. And because this consciousness beyond individuality so completely transcends our experience, the Mandukya defines it almost wholly by negatives: "invisible, inapprehensible, ungraspable, indistinguishable, unimaginable, unindicable," adding the one positive indication: "whose essence is realization of oneness with the Eternal."

The second part of the Mandukya covers the same ground. Its purpose is, to correlate what has been said with the syllable Om; to show how the sacred syllable Om carries in itself the concentrated meaning of the whole teaching. The Sanskrit word translated "syllable" means "that which cannot be diminished, that which is imperishable."

This is the Divine Self referred to the sacred syllable, the Om according to its measures; the stages are the measures, and the measures are the stages: a-u-m.

Standing in waking consciousness, Common-to-all-men, is the sound a: the first measure, from obtaining (apti) and from being first (adi-mattva). He indeed obtains all his desires, he is first, who thus knows.

Standing in dream, Radiant, is the sound u: the second measure, from exalting (utkarsha) and from being intermediate (ubhayatva). He indeed exalts the continuity of wisdom, he becomes unified, nor in his family is any born not knowing the Eternal, who thus knows.

Standing in dreamlessness, the Wise Seer, is the sound m: the third measure, from overcoming (miti) or from entering (apiti). He indeed Overcomes this world and becomes the entrance, who thus knows.

Without measure is the fourth, inapprehensible, where going forth is ended, benign, beyond duality. Thus Om is the Divine Self. Through the Self he enters into the Divine Self, who thus knows.

Perhaps the only comment needed is that the Sanskrit words in brackets (apti, utkarsha, miti), which have as their initials the three letters: a-u-m, are in part mnemonics. It would be difficult to find exact English equivalents beginning with these letters, therefore no attempt has been made to do this.

The Mandukya Upanishad is the theme of many commentaries and explanatory treatises. It is evident that its full meaning can be understood only through growth, development, spiritual experience, in which the higher realms of consciousness are unveiled. The whole substance of the great Upanishads may be used to illumine this little treatise; and it is the virtue of the Upanishads, that they have much to say concerning the higher realms of consciousness.

The Mandukya Upanishad thus gives us an outline map of four realms or ranges of consciousness. Without doubt each of the realms has within it endless diversity; perhaps we may think of each as having seven degrees, and of these again as subdivided.

Taking this outline map of consciousness, it would be profoundly interesting to inquire into the knowledge of each realm which has been recorded by the saints and mystics of the world, as something actually experienced.

For the great Christian saints, for example, we have the materials ready to hand in such a book as *The Graces of Interior Prayer*, A Treatise on Mystical Theology, by Auguste Poulain; mystical theology being the accepted term for the study of these higher states of consciousness.

For another field of spiritual experience, such a book as *The Mystics of Islam*, by Reynold A. Nicholson, will give us abundant material.

Or we may take the New Testament, finding in what Paul says of the spiritual body a commentary on what is here said of the vesture called the Radiant. So the phrase, "whose essence is realization of oneness with the Eternal" suggests the saying of the Master Christ, "I and the Father are one." And when in the words, "Before Abraham was, I am," Christ speaks of the past as the present, or of the future as the present, "I am with you always, even unto the end of the world," we have the record of a consciousness which, in the words of the Mandukya, "surpasses the three times."

Thus we may use this outline map in preparation for our journey.

NATURAL PSYCHICAL AND SPIRITUAL BODIES

Gaudapada's Poem on Mandukya Upanishad

Translated from the Sanskrit with an Interpretation

By Charles Johnston

PART I: INTRODUCTION

The shortest of all the older Upanishads is the Mandukya. Yet in some ways it contains fuller and deeper teaching than any other of these wonderful treatises of the Mysteries. For the theme of the Mandukya is the four degrees of consciousness, the Natural, the Psychical, the Spiritual, and the Divine, which make up the whole range of life, both manifested and unmanifested. And, further, to systematize and condense the teaching, and to sum it up in a single word, the Mandukya Upanishad goes on to compare the four degrees of consciousness with the four divisions of the mystical syllable "OM," which is resolved into its elements, A, U, M, thus representing both the One, and its three lower degrees of manifestation.

On this marvelous little treatise, the condensed essence of the Mystery Teaching, a certain sage, Gaudapada by name, has written a poem. This poem is now translated, prefaced by the Mandukya Upanishad itself. Gaudapada, it would seem, belongs to the period immediately after the long life-time of

Siddhartha the Compassionate, known to his devotees as Gautama Buddha, who was born at Kapilavastu five-and-twenty centuries ago. That the teachings of the Buddha were still recent, when Gaudapada wrote his poem, is shown by the way he discusses and controverts certain Nihilistic expressions of these teachings, in the latter part of his poem. The date of the work is further fixed in the period immediately after the Buddha, if the tradition of the Brahmans of Southern India be a true one, that Gaudapada is no other than Patanjali, author of the famed Yoga Sutras, and also of a learned work on Grammar. Whether we accept this tradition or no, and for my part I am inclined to believe it, we may say that the two works, the present poem and the Yoga Sutras, do fit wonderfully together, supplementing each other in a marvelous way.

And indeed it is largely the hope and expectation of translating the Yoga Sutras of Patanjali that have led me to the present work; for Patanjali plunges at once into the middle of the most practical psychology, assuming in his readers a knowledge of the spiritual philosophy of ancient India, which few modern readers, perhaps, possess. So that it is largely with the idea of supplying a philosophical and intellectual background for the Yoga Sutras of Patanjali, that I have decided to try to turn Gaudapada's poem into English. Its philosophical quality is excellent; its authority is universally accepted; and it is by no means such difficult reading as the Yoga Sutras; in fact, there is not very much in Gaudapada's poem that requires a commentary. It was, seemingly, written as a popular work, to make more readily available the summed up wisdom of the Mandukya Upanishad.

Now a word as to the position of this poem, from another point of view. It stands between the Vedic works and the Sutras of Patanjali, in date, in content, and in purpose. The older Vedic works, including the Upanishads, had, as their purpose, a consecrated life, a life permeated with the active spirit of religion, in which every part of life, every thought, word and deed, should be done "as to the Lord." The life built up on this Vedic teaching, and followed by a very large part of the people of ancient India, is hardly to be excelled in the purity of its ideal, its fervor, its value as spiritual discipline, by any like culture in the world; and this searching, stringent, spiritual culture is taken for granted, in all philosophical works, such as the present.

That, therefore, is the background of the present poem: a thorough training in practical religion, covering every detail of life, and filled with the spirit of devotion to the Most High. And after this poem come the Yoga Sutras of Patanjali, the essence of practical transcendental psychology. This helps us to define the position and purpose of the poem itself.

When the whole nature has been thoroughly trained in practical religion, and enkindled with the spirit of devotion, the time is approaching when the higher degrees of consciousness may be practically explored. The first two of these higher degrees have recently been described by Sr Oliver Lodge as "the stratum of dream," and the "stratum of genius." The "strata of dream and genius," thus described, correspond exactly to the degrees of psychical and spiritual consciousness, of the present poem; and it is marvelous how close Sir Oliver Lodge comes, both in thought and in expression, to the ancient Oriental teaching, just as he does, in his view of "the One Life, manifesting itself in the lives"; a phrase which may be claimed either by Sir Oliver or by the authors of the Prashna Upanishad. There are further degrees of consciousness, at least suspected by Sir Oliver Lodge and his colleagues, and clearly defined in the Upanishads, and in poems like the present, which follow the wisdom of the Upanishads. And these, too, must in time be entered.

But before this practical transcendental psychology can be learned, there must come a thorough and searching training of the intellect, just as the moral nature has previously been trained by practical religion. For ancient India never made the mistake of imagining that a sound training of the intellect can precede, or dispense with, a right moral training. And it is precisely to give this thorough intellectual training, built on the foundation of a consecrated religious life, that the present poem was written. It takes up, and develops, every faculty of the mind and understanding, and brings each faculty into unity with the intuitional and spiritual nature. In this way a quality of spiritual intellect is attained, which can hardly be equalled throughout the world; and the wisdom of India is perhaps most of all distinguished by this, that it adds to a perfectly religious and devoted spirit and an active spiritual will, an intellect, clear, crystalline, powerful, which grasps, and grasps successfully, the most difficult problems of thought. Such an intellect, instead of being a hindrance to spiritual attainment, may be a very powerful help; provided always it is realized that it should rest on a profoundly religious nature, and that it should be the stepping stone to practical experience of the higher degrees of consciousness, "the strata of dream and genius," and the further degrees that lie beyond; that it should stand between the devotion, let us say, of the Bhagavad Gita, and the practical transcendental psychology of such a book as the Yoga Sutras of Patanjali.

Now to turn to the poem itself. Though it is so lucid in form and style that it hardly needs a commentary, yet a very excellent commentary exists, by no less a teacher than the great Shankara himself. From this admirably conceived treatise, which is too voluminous to translate in full here, I may, perhaps, gather a few of the most interesting passages, beginning with what Shankara says, of the Mandukya Upanishad itself.

After a general introduction, Shankara proceeds to pick up difficult or technical points in the Upanishad, or in Gaudapada's poem. Thus the "sevenfold form" of the Natural Body consists of the head, the upper and lower trunk, and the arms and legs. It also refers to such characteristics as the seven plexuses. The "nineteen mouths" are the five powers of perception (what we call the five senses), the five powers of action, the five vital ethers, and the four mental powers: namely, manas, buddhi, chitta and ahankara, which we may translate emotion, intellect, imagination, and egoism. The Psychical Body is similarly formed.

Of the Psychical Consciousness, Shankara says: "The realm of the Psychical Self is dream-consciousness. In waking consciousness, with its several powers of perception, objects are perceived externally, though they are really due only to the play of Manas. Thereby impressions are imprinted on Manas. In this way Manas becomes like a canvas on which pictures are painted. Then, without external instruments, and through the action of Avidya and Kama (entranced desire), a condition similar to that of waking arises."

Of the condition of Dreamless Consciousness, Shankara writes: "In the Spiritual Consciousness, the sense of separateness ceases. It is a pure, uniform, blissful Consciousness. The Spiritual Self knows both past and future, and is therefore fitly called all-knowing." Shankara then presses home what is said of the Fourth Consciousness, the Divine, and adds: "The Fourth is attained by merging the other three into it, each degree being merged in that which is above it." Thus the Natural Self will be merged in the Psychical Self; this will be merged in the Spiritual Self; and this finally in the Divine Self, in whom all worlds rest.

Shankara has certain quaint images to illustrate the power of Maya and its relation to the Real. A rope is lying on the ground, he says; a man, seeing it indistinctly, believes it to be a snake. So is the world of illusion perceived in the Real. But there is no snake there at all; so it cannot be said to have a beginning, nor can it be said to come to an end. It simply does not exist. So is it with the illusion of a world of pain, separate from the Divine. Again, the world-illusion is like the robber imagined by the belated wayfarer, who sees a post in the twilight. When he sees that it is really a post, and no robber, it cannot be said that the robber has come to an end. There simply was no robber. So also with the mirage, the lake fancied in the salt desert, which, in Sanskrit has the pretty name of "the thirst of the deer." The images of the sun in bubbles, the sparks of the fire, the spider spinning a web from his own entrails, are others of Shankara's similes.

One he uses, which has a special interest, in these days of "hypnotic suggestion;" "A juggler," he tells us, "throws the end of a rope into the sky, and climbing up the rope, disappears with all his trappings. Then his body falls piecemeal, as though cut up by a sword, and he again comes together in the sight of the onlookers, who do not pay heed to the real nature of the illusion. In exactly the same way, the conditions of waking, dream, dreamlessness, are like the rope thrown up by the juggler who appears to climb up the rope. The real cause of the illusion stands there, apart from both the rope and him who climbs up the rope, hid by the glamor he casts, invisible. So the Fourth Consciousness, the Divine, the transcendental reality, stands apart. Therefore those noble ones who seek Liberation pay heed to the Real only, and not to the illusion that is spread before them."

This is a very famous trick, which has delighted and astonished the men of many lands, through many centuries; but only in this treatise of the great Shankara, I think, is its true nature described. There are many more admirable and luminous things in Shankara's commentary, but the limitations of time and space, as he himself would say, preclude my quoting further.

PART II: MANDUKYA UPANISHAD

"OM": This imperishable syllable is all that is. Its expansive expression is: What has been, What is, What shall be. All this is "OM." And whatever else there is, beyond the threefold division of Time, that, also, verily, is "OM." For all this is Brahma, the Eternal; and the Self, Atma, is the Eternal. And this Self stands in four worlds.

In the world of Waking Consciousness, Jagrat, objectively perceiving, of sevenfold form, with nineteen mouths—organs of sense and action—an enjoyer of gross matter, this is the Natural Self, Vaishvanara, the first measure or foot.

In the world of Dream Consciousness, Swapna, subjectively perceiving, of sevenfold form, with nineteen mouths—organs of sense and action—an enjoyer of finer matter, this is the Psychical Self, Taijasa, the second measure or foot.

Where, entered into rest, he desires no desire and beholds no dream, this is Dreamless Consciousness, Sushupti. Dreamless consciousness, unified, collective perception, verily, made of bliss, an enjoyer of bliss, perceiving through the heart, this is the Spiritual Self, Prajna, the third measure or foot. This is the All-lord, this is the all-knower, this is the Inner ruler, this is the womb of all, the forthcoming and indrawing of beings.

Neither subjectively perceiving, nor objectively perceiving, nor perceiving in both ways, neither collective perception, nor perception nor non-perception; unseen, not to be apprehended, not to be grasped, without sign of separation, unimaginable, unindicable, the essence of the consciousness of the Self, in which the manifest world ceases, full of peace, benign, secondless, this is held to be the Fourth Consciousness, this is the Self, Atma, this is the goal of wisdom.

This Self, Atma, corresponds according to syllables with the "OM" according to its measures. The measures are as the feet, and the feet are as the measures: A, U and M, to wit.

The Natural Self in Waking Consciousness, is the A, the first measure, so called from being the first, and from acquiring. He passes beyond all desires and becomes first, who thus knows,

The Psychical Self, in Dream Consciousness, is the U, the second measure, so called from its up-raising and uniting. He is upraised to the highest knowledge, and becomes united, nor in his family do knowers of the Eternal fail, who thus knows.

The Spiritual Self in Dreamless Consciousness, is the M, the third measure, so called because it measures all, or because all merges in it. He measures all, and in him all merges, who thus knows.

Without measure is the Fourth, not to be apprehended, wherein manifestation comes to rest, the benign, secondless. Thus the "OM" is as the Self, Mind. Through the Self, he enters the Self, who thus knows, who thus knows.

PART III:

GAUDAPADA'S POEM ON THE MANDUKYA UPANISHAD

PART I

Objectively perceiving, wide-extending is the Natural Self; subjectively perceiving is the Psychical Self; collectively perceiving is the Spiritual Self; the One Self, verily, is thus manifested as three.

The Natural Self has its center in the right eye, and the mouth; the Psychical Self is centered in the mental and emotional nature; in the pure ether and in the heart dwells the Spiritual Self; thus it dwells in its vesture threefold.

The Natural Self is the enjoyer of gross matter; the Psychical Self is the enjoyer of finer matter; the Spiritual Self is the enjoyer of bliss. Learn thus the threefold division of feasts.

The gross gratifies the Natural Self; the finer gratifies the Psychical Self; but bliss delights the Spiritual Self. Know thus the threefold order of delights.

He who knows both what is enjoyed in the three dwellings of the Self, and also who is the enjoyer, he, indeed, even though enjoying, shall not be stained.

The forth-coming of all beings from what has been before is certain; the One Life, the Spirit, causes each fragment of consciousness to be born.

Some who ponder on manifestation think that all comes forth by evolution; by others manifestation is deemed to be of the nature of dream or glamor.

Some think of manifestation that it is manifested through the mere will of the Lord. Those who believe in Time, think the evolution of beings comes through Time alone.

Some think all things were manifested for enjoyment; others that all was made for sport. But the universe is the very being of God; and what desire could there be in Him, who has attained all desires?

Master of the surcease of all pain, the Lord who passes not away, secondless, the God of all beings,—this is the Fourth degree of consciousness, the Divine.

The bonds of cause and what is caused rule the Natural and Psychical Selves. The Spiritual Self is bound by cause; but these two rule not in the Fourth degree of consciousness, the Divine.

The Spiritual Self perceives not beings divided into Self and Others, nor divided into the real and the inverted image of reality. The Fourth degree of consciousness, the Divine, forever beholds the All.

Divine Spiritual Self and the Divine Self have this in common, that neither perceives duality. The seed of the illusion of separateness dwells in the Spiritual Self, but no longer exists in the Divine.

Dream-forms and the illusion of separateness condition both the Natural and the Psychical Selves; the Spiritual Self has the seed of separateness without the forms of dream; but those who are established in the Fourth degree of consciousness, the Divine, perceive neither the illusion of separateness nor the forms of dream.

Through the forms of dream, things are seen as other than they are; through the illusion of separateness, one knows not the Real. When these two inversions of perception are overcome, then one enters the Fourth degree of consciousness, the Divine.

When the individual Life is awakened from the dream of beginningless world-glamor, then the unborn, undeluded, undreaming, secondless Divine is known.

If the manifest world had real being, it should pass away in time. But this duality is sheer illusion; transcendental being is one and secondless.

If the world were built up by anyone, that building should pass away in time. This expression of duality lasts only while instruction lasts; when the truth is known, duality comes to an end.

The Natural Self and the letter A have this in common, that they stand at the beginning; they have also in common the power of acquiring.

The Psychical Self and the letter U have in common the power of up-raising; they are also brought together by having the power of uniting.

The Spiritual Self is connected with the letter M through the power of measuring; through the power of merging, it is also united with it.

He who knows certainly that which is the quality in common, in the three dwellings of the Self, he is to be honored of all beings; he is to be praised as a perfect seer.

The letter A leads to the Natural Self, the letter U leads to the Psychical Self; the letter M again to the Spiritual Self; there is no going in that which is without measure.

The "OM" should be known as according with the four realms of consciousness; for without doubt these four realms correspond to the measures of "OM." When one has understood the "OM" as according with the realms of consciousness, thought need go no further.

Let him bring his consciousness to union in the sacred syllable "OM"; for the "OM" is the fearless Eternal. He who is ever united in the "OM" sees no fear anywhere.

The "OM" is the manifest Eternal, and the unmanifest Eternal also. The "OM" has nought before it, nought within it, nought without it, it passes not away.

For the "OM" is the beginning of all things, it is likewise the middle and the end. Knowing thus the "OM," he straightway enters that Supreme.

Let him know the "OM" as the Master, dwelling in the heart of every being. Understanding the "OM" as the all-embracing, the wise man sorrows no more.

By whom the "OM," the measureless, the immeasurable, the surcease of duality, the benign, is rightly known, he indeed, and no other, is the silent seer.

PART IV:

GAUDAPADA'S POEM ON THE MANDUKYA UPANISHAD

PART II

The wise have declared that all forms seen in dream are unsubstantial; because they are subjective, and not formed of gross matter. One does not actually go to the places he beholds in dream, for the time is too short; and on awaking, he does not find himself in the place he was dreaming of.

The Scripture also declares that chariots and horses seen in dream are unreal, as logic has shown. Therefore it is proven that things seen in dreams are unsubstantial.

It is taught that all things separate from the Self, though seen in waking life, are as unreal as things seen in dream. They are distinguished from these only because dreams are subjective, and of finer stuff.

The sages have declared that things seen in dream and waking are equally unreal, because both are separate from the Self, and nought but the Self is real.

That which is nothing in the beginning, and nothing at the end, is likewise nothing in the middle. Separate things are like the mirage, though they are viewed as real, not as mirage.

The efficiency of these things ceases in dream; therefore, as they have both beginning and end, they are declared to be unreal.

That dream-scenes appear in unprecedented forms, is due only to the character of him who is in the dream-condition; just as the unprecedented scenes of the heaven-world arise from the character of those in the heaven-world. He who goes there, views these things and understands them, just as one well-taught here understands what he views.

In the dream-condition, also, that which is perceived subjectively is recognized as unreal, but that which appears objectively is held to be real; yet both are equally illusory.

So in the waking condition, what is perceived subjectively is recognized as unreal, but what is grasped objectively is held to be real; yet it is fitting to hold both equally illusory.

If in both these conditions, we admit the illusory nature of all things seen as separate, who is it that thinks them separate? Who is the creator of these forms?

The Self, Atma, of Himself makes Himself appear in these forms, as a God, by his magical power of glamor. It is He who thinks these forms separate from Himself. This is the certain teaching of the Vedanta.

He as Lord molds the various forms that are ranged in subjective consciousness; it is He also who builds up the forms that are set in external consciousness.

The forms that exist only in the time that we are conscious of them in thought, and the forms that appear externally at two different times, are all equally built up by imagination; they are of different degrees, but not otherwise different.

Subjective forms which are not outwardly manifested, and things which are clearly seen as external, are all alike built by the imagination; the only difference between them is the difference of the powers which perceive them.

The Self, Atma, first forms the Individual Life, Jiva; thereafter the Self shapes beings of varied form, both those which are external, and those which are in self-consciousness. According to the inherent knowledge of the Individual Life, so is its memory.

As the rope, which cannot be perceived distinctly in the dark, is changed by imagination into various forms, such as a serpent, or a streak of water, so is the Self, Atma, changed by imagination into various forms.

As the imagined form vanishes when the rope is distinctly seen, and it is perceived that there is the rope, and nothing else, so is the clear perception of the Self, Atma.

The Self is imagined to take the forms of the life-breaths and numberless other forms; this is the magical glamor of the God, whereby Himself is concealed from view.

Those who believe in the Life see Him as Life; those who believe in the elements see Him as the elements; those who believe in the Nature-powers see Him as the Nature-powers; those who believe in the forms of matter, see Him as the forms of matter.

Those who see the four degrees of consciousness, perceive Him as the four stages of consciousness; those who believe in objects, see Him as objects; those who believe in worlds, see Him as worlds; those who believe in Gods, see Him as the Gods.

Those who believe in the Scriptures, the Vedas, see Him in the Scriptures; those who believe in sacrifices, see Him in sacrifices; those who think of the consciousness which enjoys, see Him as the enjoying consciousness; those who think of what is enjoyed, see Him as what is enjoyed.

Those whose thought is set on the subtle, see Him as the subtle; those whose thoughts are set on the gross, see Him as the gross; those who think of the formed, see Him in the formed; those who think of the formless, see Him in the formless.

Those who think of Time, see Him as Time; those who think of space, see Him in space; those who are set on words, think of Him as words; those who dwell on the worlds, think of Him as the worlds. Those who dwell on emotion, think of Him as emotion; those who dwell on pure thought, think of Him as pure thought; those who dwell in imagination, think of Him as imagination; those who dwell in law, think of Him as Law; those who disregard law, think of Him as above law.

Some see Him as the five-and-twenty powers, others as the six-and-twenty; others as one-and-thirty; yet others as innumerable.

Those who think of the realms of life, declare Him to be the regions of life; those who think of the stages of development, see Him as the stages of development; those who think of difference of sex, think of Him as feminine, masculine, neuter; others think of Him as the Higher and the Lower.

Those who believe in evolution, think of Him as evolution; those who believe in involution, think of Him as involution; those who believe the world is stationary, think of Him as stationary. Thus all ever perceive Him, each after his own thought.

In whatever form He may appear to anyone, that form each beholds; He protects him, becoming that form; and he who thinks on Him under that form, enters into Him.

He, who is not divided, appears divided through these various forms; he who knows this truly, may without fear imagine Him in any form.

As a dream or an illusion of glamor, or as fairy-city seen in the air, such is all this world declared to be, by the seers, in the Vedanta teachings.

There is no coming to an end, there is no manifestation, there is none bound, there is none seeking to attain, there is none seeking freedom, there is none freed, this is the transcendental, the final truth.

By Him, though ever One, this is imagined in unreal forms; the forms are all produced by the One; therefore Oneness is the blessed state.

These varied forms are not of the same nature as the Self, nor are they of independent nature; they have no being either separate from the Self, or not separate from the Self; thus have the knowers of the Real perceived.

By those from whom passion and fear and wrath are gone, the Masters of silence, who have crossed to the farther shore of the Vedas, is this Unchanging One beheld, in whom the worlds come to surcease, who is secondless.

Therefore, knowing Him thus, let him fix his memory on the Secondless One; gaining the Secondless One, let him walk the world as though it were inert.

Let him who has conquered himself be above praise, seeking no adoration, ceasing from offerings to spirits; though amid the mutable, yet dwelling in the immutable; meeting the events of life as they come.

Seeing the reality beneath self-consciousness, and seeing also the reality beneath external things, let him become the reality, finding his pleasure-ground therein, never falling below the Real.

PART V:

INTRODUCTION TO PART III

The part of Gaudapada's poem translated in the present number is so lucid, so simple, so convincing, that any comment on it seems superfluous. Nevertheless, great men have commented on it, and among them even the great Shankara. Therefore we cannot refuse humbly to follow in the great Shankara's footsteps.

Let us begin by reminding our readers of the position of Gaudapada's poem, both chronological and logical. First, as to the personality of Gaudapada. He was, the tradition of Southern India tells us, no other than the sage whom we know as Patanjali, author of the famed Yoga Sutras. And this work, as we understand it, was intended to bridge, and does in fact bridge, the chasm between such splendid works of the prime, as the Mandukya Upanishad, and the closely technical system of the Yoga School, with its precise, practical instructions for duly qualified students. Students who are to approach the Yoga Sutras with some hope of mastering them, need, as we have already seen, two kinds of powers or qualifications. First, the moral powers, the quiet heart, the well-ruled nature, the awakened will, which does all things as to the Master, and the ardent flame of aspiration. Hardly less needful is the clear intellect, the lucid insight, well-poised, swift, luminous. And it is, if we rightly understand the question, chiefly to the end of training the intellect, and endowing it with just such powers, that Gaudapada wrote his famous poem; and that the great Shankara enriched it with the treasures of his peerless, matchless lucidity. No spirit more transparent ever gave forth the Indian Wisdom; and with his clear and critical genius, Shankara is ever the poet, the worshipper.

The present chapter of the poem, the third, seeks to awaken and to strengthen in the understanding a deep realization of the oneness of the individual soul with the universal Soul. And once that realization is reached, the intellect has laid the foundations of lasting sanity. It is of interest to every student of comparative religion and philosophy to find that, just about the time when Gaudapada's poem was written in distant India, Empedocles was thinking his way to like conclusions in the bright land of Hellas, or at least within the realm illumined by Grecian light. Take, for instance, the twentieth and following verses of Gaudapada's poem: "Some would have it that the unborn, everlasting Being comes to birth. But how could the unborn, the immortal, come to mortality? The immortal becomes not mortal, nor does mortal become immortal;" and compare them with the verses of Empedocles:

> More will I tell thee too: there is no birth
> Of all things mortal, nor end in ruinous death;
> But mingling only and interchange of mixed
> There is, and birth is but its name with men. . .
> But when in man, wild beast, or bird, or bush,
> These elements commingle and arrive
> The realms of light, the thoughtless deem it "birth";
> When they dispart, 'tis "doom of death"; and though
> Not this the Law, I too assent to use. . .
> Fools! for their thoughts are briefly brooded o'er.
> Who trust that what is not can e'er become,

Or aught that is can wholly die away.
From what-is-not what-is can ne'er become;
So that what-is should e'er be all destroyed,
No force could compass and no ear hath heard—
For there 'twill be forever where 'tis set. . .
The All hath neither Void nor overflow. . .
But with the All there is no Void, so whence
Could aught of more come nigh?. . .
No wise man dreamed such folly in his heart,
That only whilst we live what men call life
We have our being and take our good and ill,
And ere as mortals we compacted be,
And when as mortals we be loosed apart,
We are as nothing. . .
Behold those elements own equal strength
And equal origin; each rules its task;
And unto each its primal mode; and each

Prevailing conquers with revolving time.
And more than these there is no birth nor end;
For were they wasted ever and evermore,
They were no longer, and the great All were then
How to be plenished, and from what far coast?
And how, besides, might they to ruin come,
Since nothing lives that empty is of them?
No, these are all, and, as they course along
Through one another, now this, now that is born—
And so forever down Eternity. . .

So far Empedocles. We need not point out that his conception is more objective, that of Gaudapada more interior and mystical. Yet Empedocles also rises to heights of mysticism, as when he hymns the One in words truly Indian in spirit, though Greek in form:

> We may not bring It near us with our eyes,
> We may not grasp It with our human hands...
> For 'tis adorned with never a manlike head,
> For from Its back there swing no branching arms,
> It hath no feet nor knees alert; It lives
> One holy Mind, ineffable, alone,
> And with swift thoughts darts through the universe...

And even more genuinely Indian in both thought and word is his final vision of things to come, when Patience' perfect work shall have been accomplished, and mankind shall be regenerate:

> And seers at last, and judges of high hymns,
> Physicians sage, and chiefs o'er earth-born men
> Shall they become, whence germinate the gods,
> The excellent in honors.

> And we shall have once more a divine humanity, which shall abide

> At hearth and feast companioned with the immortals,
> From human pains and wasting eld immune.

Such an identity of thought and expression leads us to give greater credence to the old tradition that from India as well as from Egypt the mysteries came to Hellas; and that the Greek sages, when they put forth what our scholars term speculative philosophies, are in reality giving forth, in guarded terms, in symbol and metaphor, the pristine teachings of the Mysteries. With this preface, we take up again the translation of Gaudapada's poem.

PART VI:

GAUDAPADA'S POEM ON THE MANDUKYA UPANISHAD

PART III

One takes refuge in devotion, thinking that he has been evolved by the Creator, and that before this evolution nothing was; such a one is deemed of mean understanding.

Therefore I shall tell of that which is beyond mean understanding, which enters not into birth, which is forever equal; since, though seeming to enter into birth, this is not born at all.

The Supreme Self is likened to space, which is made up of the sum of spaces enclosed in jars, and includes the jars also. This is the best simile for evolution.

When the jars and other containing vessels are destroyed, the spaces that were contained in the jars and the like melt into universal Space. So individual selves melt into the infinite Self.

Just as, when the space contained in any jar is soiled by dust and smoke, the space contained in other jars is not soiled. So all individual selves are not affected by the happiness or sorrow of one individual self.

Everywhere there is difference of form and nature and name. But there is not therefore any difference in Space. This again is a simile of the Universal Self.

Just as the space contained in a jar is neither a separated part nor an evolved effect, of Space, so likewise the individual self is neither a separated part or an evolved effect of the Self.

As space, in the thought of the inexperienced child, seems stained, so does the Self seem to be stained, to those who are unawakened. As far as dying, being born, going and coming are concerned, in the case of all beings it is just as in the case of Space.

All separate beings are like the creatures of a dream, sent forth by the glamor-power of the Supreme Self. Their relations, of greater and less, or of equals, are no proof that they are real.

For the substance of the Five Veils of the Self, enumerated in the Taittiriya Upanishad, is of the Highest Being, as in the illustration of the portions of space, and Space.

In the contrasted terms of the Teaching of Nectar, the oneness of the Supreme Eternal is taught; just as Space is one, whether it be the space contained in the earth, or in the body of man.

The unity of the individual soul and the universal Soul is proclaimed. The thought of diversity between them is reproved. Therefore their oneness is the truth.

The description of the individual soul and the universal Soul as separate before the growth of the soul is attained, is only to make intelligible the growth of the soul. It does not represent a reality.

Similes for the Soul, taken from clay that can be molded, from iron that can be welded, from sparks that come forth from the flame, are different in character. They are but means for the understanding to pass over. There is no real division at all.

As there are three stages of life, the lower, the middle and the higher, so there are three stages of vision. This way of devotion is taught for the sake of attaining these.

Those who believe the individual soul is separate from the universal Soul, each set firm in his own opinion, are in conflict with each other. But this teaching of Oneness is in conflict with none.

For the teaching of Oneness is the transcendental Truth, and duality is a part of it. As they also teach duality, this Truth does not conflict with them.

The Eternal, ever unborn, appears to be divided through Glamor only, for, were the division real, the immortal would take on mortality.

Some would have it that the unborn, everlasting Being comes to Birth. But how could the unborn, the immortal, come to mortality?

The immortal becomes not mortal, nor does the mortal become immortal. For nothing can become the contrary of its own nature. If any think that what of its own nature is immortal can come to mortality, how can he hold that it stands immortal and changeless? The Scripture holds the same teaching regarding birth, whether that birth be real or unreal; that alone is certain which is taught by Scripture and affirmed by reason.

Such sentences of Scripture as that which declares "There is no separateness," and "Indra, through glamor, appeared as manifold;" prove that He, the ever unborn, appears to be born through Glamor alone.

The sentence of Scripture, which forbids worship of the Formative Power, proves that the Formative Power is not final Reality. And the sentence, "Who can bring Him into birth?" proves that causation is not final Reality.

"It is not that, not that!" This sentence denies all properties in the Self. The Real is sought to be indicated by sheer incomprehensibility.

The birth of the Real is perceived only through Glamor; it is not a reality. He for whom the Real is really born, must think of it as perpetually reborn.

The Unreal never enters birth, whether in reality or through Glamor; just as the son of the barren woman is never born, whether really or in seeming.

As in dream the mind divides itself into the seer and the thing seen through the power of Glamor, in just the same way the mind, in waking, divides itself into the seer and the things seen, through the power of Glamor.

As the mind, which is really not divided, appears as divided in dream; in just the same way the Mind, really not divided, appears as divided in waking.

Whatever division there is, among things animate or inanimate, is an appearance of the Mind's making. When Mind transcends mind, no division any longer exists.

When by awakening to the reality of the Self, the mind's imaginings are brought to rest, then does Mind transcend mind, ceasing to grasp after externals, since naught is left, other than Self, for it to grasp.

The true knowing is declared to be free from imaginings, and not separate from what is known; the Eternal, unborn, everlasting, is what is known; by the unborn the unborn is comprehended.

The condition of the mind which has transcended itself, which is free from imaginings and has reached wisdom, is beyond the condition of dreamless sleep, and different from it.

For in dreamless sleep the mind has simply sunk into quiescence; but when Mind transcends mind it has not simply sunk into quiescence, but has entered completely into the realm of wisdom, the fearless Eternal.

Unborn, beyond drowsiness, beyond dream, beyond both name and form, shining out all at once, all knowledge, beyond the need of specific forms of service.

It has passed beyond all descriptive speech, it has risen above all forms of imagination; it has entered into peace, it is all at once full of light, it is pure vision, unmoved and fearless.

Where no form is perceived by the thought, there is naught to grasp nor to surrender; then the power of knowing has come to rest in the Self. Reaching perfect being, it knows no further birth.

The union with the intangible is hard to perceive for the seekers of union; the seekers of union draw back in fear from That, seeing fear where there is no fear.

The seekers of union think that on perfect control of the mind depend freedom from fear, the conquest of pain, awakening to the light, and everlasting peace.

Just as it is possible to empty the ocean, by picking it up drop by drop on the tip of a blade of kusha grass, so it is possible completely to control the mind by infinite perseverance.

By the right means one should gain control over the mind, whether it be scattered abroad after the feasts of desire, or sunk down in sluggish sloth; for lust and sloth are equal dangers.

Let him turn the mind back from lust by holding in memory the pain of all perishing things; for remembering that all is unborn, he ceases to perceive what is manifest through birth.

Let the mind that is sunk in sloth be awakened; let the mind that is scattered be brought back to peace. Let him know that the mind is prone to unrest and lust; therefore, when it has gained peace, let him keep it in peace.

Let him not allow it to hold with relish to the happiness of this peace, but let him through spiritual vision break free from all attachment. Let him by effort of will bring the mind to oneness with the Self, keeping it poised, in perfect stillness.

When the mind sinks not back in sloth, and scatters itself no more abroad, no longer like a flickering flame, no longer catching false reflections, then it is one with the Eternal, in perfect stillness.

Self-sustained, full of peace, entered into Nirvana, ineffable, is that most excellent joy; it is declared to be the all-knowing unborn, at one with the unborn goal of all knowing.

The individual soul is not really born; it has no real separate being; that is the highest truth, which perceives that naught is really born.

PART VII:

INTRODUCTION TO PART IV

We shall best understand the argument at the outset of this fourth installment of Gaudapada's wonderful poem, if we study the modern parallel to the ancient Indian controversy.

Gaudapada wishes to prove that the One Spirit alone is; that all else is unreal, that is, non-eternal. He finds two other doctrines in the field. The first of these declares "that the world is the manifestation of what has had previous being." Others, equally wise, declare "that it is the manifestation of what has had no previous being." These ancient disputants correspond exactly to two classes at the present day. The first, the scientists, affirm that the world is the manifestation of matter, and that matter has existed from eternity. The second, the theologians, declare that the world came into being through a creative act; that, up to a certain time, nothing at all existed, of all the vast panorama of the worlds; and that then the Creator, by an exercise of His Will, by the pronouncement of His Word, brought the universe into being. Gaudapada, like the good Vedantin he is, uses these two views to cancel each other, so that the true Vedantin teaching may be left alone in the field. He lets the two disputants demolish each other. The theologian retorts to the scientist that, if the latter explains the formation of the world from already existing matter, his explanation is no explanation at all; for he leaves out the question of how matter came into being. To say that it was always there, in one form or another, is to make a pretence at explaining, without really explaining. The scientist retorts that the theologian's idea is unthinkable; that nothing could come into being from nothing. Gaudapada smiles and rubs his hands, and admits most affably that the objections of both disputants are sound; and they bring us inevitably to the true Vedantin teaching, namely, that the whole manifested universe neither came into being from nothing, nor came into being from something that was there before; but that its existence is only a seeming, a mirage in the desert. There is no manifested universe at all. Nothing is, but the Eternal.

In like fashion, he undermines the view that the manifested universe is an externalization of the Eternal. This he deals with along the lines of formal Indian logic, by examining the relation of cause and effect. He comes practically to the conclusion of Kant, that causation is but a form of our thought, a colored window through which we view the colorless Real; causation, like time and space, is in our thought, not in the Thing-in-Itself, the Real. So is the sage of Königsberg anticipated by two milleniums. "Therefore there is no external manifestation either of objects or of the mind. They who see such a thing are looking at something as non-existent, as a footprint in the sky."

The argument from the unreality of dreams, in the verses which follow, is full of humor. Gaudapada almost exactly anticipates the famous Scot, who dreamed a most delicious and appetizing haggis, but unfortunately omitted to dream a spoon.

Equally humorous, equally modern, is the elephant of the fortieth verse. We may imagine Gaudapada chuckling to think of one of his opponents being chased by an imaginary elephant, conjured up by hypnotic suggestion. The simile of the fire-brand whirled in the air, which is introduced at the forty-seventh verse, is peculiarly charming. I suppose we have all, in the days of happy childhood, taken a stick, burned its end to a red ember, and then whirled it in the dark, weaving lovely circles of fire through the blackness, or tracing red zig-zags and ovals against the night. This simile has, indeed, given this section of the poem its title: The Quenching of the Fire-brand; and what follows is so lucid as to need no comment or explanation.

PART VIII:

GAUDAPADA'S POEM ON THE MANDUKYA UPANISHAD

PART IV

"QUENCHING OF THE FIRE-BRAND"

He who, by wisdom clear and wide as the ether, illumining through union with what is known, has realized that all visible qualities are but as the visible sky which rests in the ether: him I praise, of men most excellent.

He who teaches the Union which is limitless, bringing happiness to all beings, beings free from dissonance or discord; to him in reverence I bow.

There are some who affirm the world is the manifestation of what has had previous being; others, as wise, declare it the manifestation of what has had no previous being. Thus they contradict each other.

But what has previous being is already manifested, object these latter. What has had no previous being can never be manifested, object the former. Thus they come to the teaching of the Advaita, which declares that manifestation is unreal.

For we gladly accept the objections to the reality of manifestation, which they thus raise. Know therefore we have no dispute with these.

There are those who wish to maintain the real manifestation of that Real, which is ever unmanifest. But how can the unmanifest, immortal Real come to mortality?

The immortal becomes not mortal, nor can the mortal become immortal. For it is impossible that anything can become the opposite of its own nature.

He who says that what is by nature immortal may become mortal—how can he maintain that what enters into manifestation nevertheless remains immortal?

The nature of a thing is that which is complete in itself, that which is its very essence, that which is innate, that which is not added to it from without, that which does not lose its inherent character.

All real beings are of their own nature free from old age and death. If they accept the thought of old age and death, they fall away from their own nature.

He who admits that the cause and the effect of life are one, believes the process of causing is the origin of manifestation. But how can the unmanifest pass into manifestation? Or how can the Eternal One be divided?

If it be meant that the effect is not of other nature than the cause, and if the cause be unmanifest, then how can the cause of an effect, which is manifest, be itself changeless?

If one assert that an effect comes into being from a cause which is unmanifested, then there is no example of this. Or if it be said that the effect springs from a cause already manifest, and this from another, then no solution is reached.

There are those who declare the result is the source of the cause, and the cause again the source of the result. How can such maintain that either cause or result is sourceless?

When they say the result is the source of the cause, and the cause again the source of the result, they assert a progression like the birth of the father from the son.

You must determine the order of cause and result in manifestation. Two things which appear simultaneously cannot be related causally, like the two horns of an ox.

A cause which has its source in a result can have no perfect being. How can a cause which is imperfect accomplish a result? If the completeness of the cause depend on the result, and the completeness of the result on the cause, which of the two comes into being before the other? For the completion of the one depends on the other.

This dilemma rests either on inability to explain, or incomplete knowledge, or the fact that the order of succession breaks down. In each case, these learned views only serve to illumine more brightly the teaching that manifestation has no real existence.

There is the illustration of the tree produced from the seed. But this is of the same nature as the relation of cause and effect. Therefore it is not fitting to use in explanation a case of the same nature as the thing to be explained.

Inability to determine which is first and which is last likewise strengthens the teaching that manifestation is unreal. For how could it be said of anything which comes into being, that its antecedent is unknowable?

We teach that no reality comes into manifestation either from itself or from any other thing. Whether it be being or non-being or both, no reality ever comes into manifestation.

The cause of the beginningless cannot come into manifestation, nor can the result come into manifestation of itself. For if anything is beginningless, then it never begins at all.

But this objection is raised; There must be a cause which gives birth to perceptions; otherwise both would cease to exist. And also from the existence of pain, the reality of external causes must be accepted.

We admit that reason demands that a cause be assigned for perception. But the nature of things equally demands that this cause shall be itself causeless.

The imagination does not come into contact with objects, nor is there a mirroring of objects in the imagination. For the object has no permanent reality, nor does the mirrored image exist apart from the object.

The imagination never touches any real object whether in past, present or future. And how could there be a mistaken impression of something that has no existence?

Therefore there is no external manifestation either of objects or of the mind. They who see such a thing are looking at something as non-existent as a footprint in the sky.

People say that the unmanifested comes into outward manifestation. But its very nature is to be unmanifested. And nothing can possibly depart from its own nature.

And it is illogical to say that the circle of birth and rebirth is beginningless, and at the same time to say that it is non-eternal. And likewise, unless Liberation be beginningless, it cannot be eternal.

That which has no being in the past, and has no being in the future, must also have no being in the present. Things which seem not to be illusions are nevertheless of like nature with illusions.

Though they seem to be means to an end, yet this seeming ceases in sleep. Therefore, as they have beginning and end, they cannot have real being.

All things beheld in dream are but mirages, for they have no existence outside the body. For how could there be a beholding of real objects in so circumscribed a space?

Nor can it be that the dreamer beholds distant things by going to them, for no time is taken in going. Nor does the dreamer find himself at the distant place when he awakes.

Though he has talked with friends in dream, he does not find them there when he awakes. Even if he has laid hold of anything, he does not find it in his hand when he wakes.

The body in which we take part in dreams is unreal, since there is still the physical body apart from it. And as is the dream body, so are all things; they are all but figments of the imagination.

Because dreams are so like waking experiences, the latter must be their cause. Therefore, it may be said, waking experiences must be real.

But we say that nothing is ever really manifested outwardly, since outward manifestation has no real existence. And further the unreal is never caused by the real.

Having experienced the unreal in waking consciousness, he who is saturated with it sees it again in dream. And having experienced the unreal in dream, the man wakes up, and sees it no longer.

It cannot be that both the unreal and the real have their cause in the unreal. Even the real cannot be said to have the real as its cause; how then could this be said of the unreal?

Just as in waking, through imaginative illusion one can seem to touch things not to be thought of as real; so in dream, through imaginative illusion, one sees things possible only in dream.

But the teaching that manifestation is a reality is put forward by the sages, only for the sake of those who are afraid of the thought that manifestation is no reality, those who rest their belief on common experience and on the adequacy of ritual acts.

Those who are afraid of the thought that manifestation is no reality, and who rely on experience, suffer no great detriment thereby, though they do fall short of truth.

As an elephant which is a mere hypnotic illusion may be the basis of experience and the cause of action, in just the same way what we call objectivity is the basis of experience and action.

The One, which is ever at peace, which is pure Consciousness, without manifestation, motion or material existence, appears to have manifestation, appears to be in motion, appears to material.

Thus, verily, neither is imagination outwardly manifested, nor are objects outwardly manifested; thus, verily, the wise fall not into these inverted illusions.

Just as a fire-brand whirled in the air appears to make straight or crooked line of light, so Consciousness set in motion gives the appearance of perceiver and perceived, subject and object.

Just as the fire-brand does not really take these shapes, but remains apart from this illusion and unchanged by it; so, verily, does Consciousness remain apart from the illusion of manifestation, and unchanged by it.

When the fire-brand is whirled about, the appearances it gives rise to, do not come from any external source; nor do they go anywhere else when it ceases to be whirled, nor do they withdraw into the firebrand.

They do not go out of the fire-brand, because they have no substantial existence; just the same is true of Consciousness, for the illusion of appearance is common to both of them.

When Consciousness is in motion, the appearances in it do not come from any external source; nor, when its motion ceases, do they go to any other place; nor do they withdraw again into consciousness.

They do not go out of Consciousness, because they have no substantial existence; they are always incapable of being accounted for by thought, because they are outside of causality.

Substance is the cause of substance; what is other than substance is the cause of what is other than substance. But conscious selves are neither substance nor other than substance.

In the same way, conscious selves are not the effect of imagination, nor is imagination the effect of conscious selves. Thus the wise take refuge in the truth that there is no real manifestation of cause and effect.

So long as there is a belief in cause and effect, so long will there be the seeming operation of cause and effect. But when the belief in cause and effect fades, then also will the seeming operation of cause and effect pass away.

So long as there is a belief in cause and effect, so long will the sequence of birth and rebirth continue; but when the belief in cause and effect fades away, the sequence of birth and rebirth will cease.

Through the enveloping power of delusion all manifestation comes into being, therefore it is not eternal. As everything is in reality not manifested, through its non-separation from the Real, therefore there is no destruction of anything.

The conscious selves that seem to come into manifestation, do not really come into manifestation. It is through Glamor that they seem to come into manifestation. And Glamor has no real being.

Just as from a seed which is the result of Glamor, a sprout which is the result of Glamor comes forth, and is neither eternal, nor subject to destruction, so is the manifestation of conscious selves.

Since conscious selves do not in reality come into manifestation, they cannot be said either to be eternal as such, or not to be eternal. Where no distinctions of quality exist, there can be no distinguishing description.

Just as in dream the imagination plays at subject and object, through the power of Glamor; in just the same way, in waking, the imagination plays at subject and object, through the power of Glamor.

And as there is no doubt at all that the imagination, which seems thus divided in dream, is not divided, so there is no doubt at all that the imagination, which seems to be dual in waking, is not really divided.

The beholder of a dream, moving about in dream in all the ten directions of space, sees all kinds of living things standing there, whether egg-born or sweat-born, or whatever they be.

But they exist only in the imagination of the beholder of the dream, and have no existence separate from him; in just the same way the imagination of the beholder of the dream has no existence apart from him.

So one who is awake moves through the ten directions of the waking world, and beholds all kinds of living things, whether egg-born or sweat-born.

But these beings are visible only to the waking consciousness, and have no existence apart from it. In just the same way, the imagination of waking consciousness has no separate existence.

The two depend for their seeming existence on their mutual interaction; both are beyond the range of every instrument of mental analysis, for such instrument exists only in them.

Just as the being seen in dream appears to pass through birth and death, so all these beings in the world neither are nor are they not.

Just as the being produced by glamor seems to pass through birth and death, so all these beings in the world neither are nor are they not.

Just as the being created by suggestion seems to pass through birth and death, so all these beings in the world neither are nor are they not.

No being is really born; there is no real manifestation for him. This is the supreme truth, which teaches that naught is really manifested.

This dual world of perceiver and perceived comes into being through the motion of the imagination. Therefore the imagination is declared to be unrelated to objects, everlasting, unattached.

The being that is built up by the enveloping power of illusion has no transcendental reality. So things held to exist by the delusions of other schools of thought, have no transcendental reality.

The Real is spoken of as unmanifest, through the illusion of defective thought, but it cannot in the transcendental sense even be said to be unmanifest. It is said to be unmanifest, only with reference to other defective schools of thought, which speak of it as manifest.

Firm faith persists only in that which does not come into being; in that, there is no duality. He who understands that duality is unreal, is beyond causation, and does not fall into birth.

Where the imagination accepts no causes, whether good, bad or middling, then it falls not into birth; for without a cause, how can there be an effect?

The non-manifestation of the imagination, which is thus without a cause, is non-dual and unconditioned; the same is true of everything unborn, for it is but the work of the imagination.

Awaking to the truth that causation is not a final reality, and finding no external, separate cause for manifested existence, one reaches the heart's desire, the resting-place that is free from fear and beyond sorrow.

Belief that unreal things are real attaches us to unreal things. But when we wake up to the fact that outer things are unreal, we become free from attachment to them.

Poise unshakable is his, who is free from the illusion of outward reality and manifestation. This is the aim of the awakened; this is the unconditioned, the unborn, the One.

The Self is unborn, free from drowsiness and dreams, self-illumined; by the very nature of its being, it is ever self-illumined.

Through our grasping after one outer object after another, the joy of the Self is perpetually concealed, and suffering fills our field of view. But the Lord, the real Self is there, awaiting us.

The childish minded fails to find the Self, because he is wrapped up in arguments as to whether it is or is not, is and is not, or exists not at all; arguments drawn from the ideas of things moving or stable or both, or non-being.

The Self is perpetually being concealed by predicating of it one of these four alternatives. He is the perfect Seer, who beholds the Self as untouched by these.

When he has attained complete omniscience, the secondless resting-place of the Eternal, which is without beginning, middle or end, what remains for him to long for?

This is the highest virtue of the twice-born, this is called the true peace, this is the true control which springs from the conquest of the lower nature; he who knows this, shall enter into peace.

"The sense of the world as dual, made up of outer things and inner emotions, is a worldly perception. The sense of the world as single, made up of emotions without outer things, is equally worldly.

That which is beyond outer things and emotions is declared to be above worldly experience; it is proclaimed by the wise to be at once wisdom, and the goal of wisdom and knowledge.

When the knowledge of the three worlds is grasped, when they are known in ascending degrees, then the sage enters into perfect knowledge of all things.

The first steps of knowledge, concerning what is to be abandoned, what is to be known, what is to be acquired, what is to be ripened, are all but figurative expressions, except that which concerns what is to be known.

All different forms and characters should be known as by nature like the ether, beginningless. Their difference is not real at any time, in any place.

All forms and characters but dwell in thought, through their very nature; from the beginning, they are clearly defined. He who accepts this truth, builds for immortality.

By their very nature, all forms and characters are devoid of true outward existence, they are essentially unreal, they have no being apart from the Self, the unborn, which brings us light.

Those who dwell in the thought of separateness do not reach the Light. Those who are in bondage to separateness, who declare that objects really exist apart from the Self, are pitiful.

But those who will dwell firm-set in the unborn One, they indeed are wise in this world; but this wisdom the world cannot reach.

True wisdom is that which, being unmanifest, does not hold itself to be dependent on forms and characters which have no real being. Wisdom, thus independent, is declared to be free from attachment.

There can be no true detachment for the unwise in whom dwells even an atom of the sense of separateness; is not this the very thing that conceals the Real?

Since all forms and characters are of their very nature one with the stainless Self, they have never been the cause of the

Self's concealment. From the beginning they are nothing but thought; they can be known, only as being nothing but thought.

The wisdom of him who has reached illumination, who is full of fervor, does not concern itself with characters and forms; for him, forms and characters have no true reality. This is not the same as saying that the subjective is real.

Having thus realized the One, which is hard to behold, which dwells in the deeps, which is ever equal, which is full of light, that resting-place where there is no separateness: let us bow down to that One, in the measure of our enlightenment.

THE END

www.ingramcontent.com/pod-product-compliance
Lightning Source LLC
LaVergne TN
LVHW041458070426
835507LV00009B/659